Aurora

Ghost City of the Dawn

AURORA, Roman name for Eos, goddess of the Dawn, is derived from the same Latin root as *Aurum*, gold. Like the dawn, the city of Aurora glowed brightly with hope and then faded into daytime reality.

By Robert E. Stewart

NEVADA PUBLICATIONS
Box 15444 • Las Vegas, Nevada 89114

THE
FRIENDS OF
BODIE

WINGATE HALL was built into the bank of the gulch on the north side of Aurora's main street. In the mid-twentieth century it stood abandoned and weathering. After the brick robbers finished in the 1950s, only a portion of the rock foundation remained.

When You Visit

Bodie State Historic Park is best visited during the summer. At other times the weather is unpredictable. Off-season visitors are cautioned to check at the Mono County Sheriff's office in Bridgeport for road and weather conditions before making the trip. Roads are often difficult; trailers are not advised. Over-snow equipment (snowmobiles, skis, snow shoes, etc.) may be required to reach the park during the winter months.

The Park is open year-round; 9:00 a.m. to 7:00 p.m. in the summer months, and 9:00 a.m. to 4:00 p.m. the rest of the year. An entrance fee is charged year-round.

For more information about Bodie State Historic Park you may contact the park either by writing to:

BODIE STATE HISTORIC PARK
Post Office Box 515
Bridgeport, California 93517
or by calling the park directly at:
(619) 647-6445

Please Help Us

- DON'T TOUCH ANYTHING: leave every rock and rusty can in place for out grandchildren to see.
- WATCH OUT: This is a real ghost town; splinters of wood, nails and broken glass are everywhere.
- DON'T SMOKE: except in the parking lot.
- The mill area is hazardous; please stay out.
- Unless otherwise noted, all buildings are closed to the public.

DEPARTMENT OF PARKS & RECREATION
State of California – The Resources Agency
P.O. Box 942896
Sacramento, CA 94296-0838

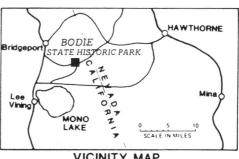

VICINITY MAP

The Friends of Bodie is a group dedicated to the preservation of the gold mining ghost town of Bodie. It is a chapter of the Tahoe-Sierra State Parks Association. This is a volunteer, non-profit organization which helps preserve and interpret state parks in the Sierra District of the State Department of Parks and Recreation.

In 1962 Bodie became a state historic park. This did not automatically insure all structures and artifacts would be properly preserved. Within the State Park System Bodie must compete with other parks for funding and priority projects. Likewise, the Department of Parks and Recreation must compete with all other state agencies for limited amounts of funding.

The Friends of Bodie can help raise funds and provide volunteer support to insure that Bodie is properly preserved.

Financial support and volunteer workers are vital in preserving Bodie. Should you wish to participate in this effort please contact:

The Friends of Bodie
Post Office Box 515
Bridgeport, California 93517

Picture Credits are as follows:

Joe Curtis Collection
  Back cover; page 36
Nevada Publications Collection
  Cover; Page 2 (Nell Murbarger photo); maps on pages 11, 19;
  photos on pages 17, 18, 34-35, 36 (both), 38-39, 40, 48
Nevada State Museum
  Photos on pages 31, 32
Central Nevada Historical Society
  Page 7, Society's Jack Manhire collection.
William Clements Library, University of Michigan
  Page 43
Author's Collection
  Pages 12, 13, 14, 33, 41 Sketches and maps, pages 13, 14, 24, 25,
  45 by the author.

FRONT COVER: Looking east along Aurora's main street, about 1925-30.

Aurora – *Ghost City of the Dawn*
© Copyright 1996, by Sierra State Parks
Foundation/Friends of Bodie.
Republication rights retained by Nevada Publications
For further information, or a catalog of 135
Southwestern books, call (702) 747-0800.

Designed at WHITE SAGE STUDIOS,
DRAWER G, Virginia City, Nevada 89440

ISBN 0-913814-81-4

Aurora

Ghost City of the Dawn

A rush of excitement flowed through the minds of three men as they realized the rock they were looking at was rich with gold and silver – a real strike!

The date was August 25, 1860. The place was in the mountains just east of Mono Lake. E.R. Hicks, J. M. Corey and James M. Braly were on a hunting and prospecting expedition. They had been traversing the Walker River area of western Utah Territory. It was midday when they found a great ore body just above a mountain meadow. Corey had recently read Victor Hugo's then-new novel *The Hunchback of Notre Dame*. They christened the region the "Esmeralda Mining District," after the heroine of the book.

The exhilaration of a new mineral discovery quickly spread to other prospectors and miners exploring east and south from Virginia City and the year-old Comstock Lode. Within days, "Esmeralda" grew into a crude mining camp, and soon it became a village.

Like an *aurora borealis* developing quickly in the sky, the town of Aurora blossomed in a meadow near that great gold strike. It shone magnificently for several years, and then faded into memory. During its short life, Aurora produced impressive amounts of gold and silver from its shallow mines, in fact, more than $30 million.

Unlike the placer mines of California's Mother Lode, the gold of Nevada was bedded in hard rock, requiring digging of deep prospect holes, tunnels, and the sinking of shafts. This important difference meant that mining would require significant capital investments, not just pick and shovel work.

In California's placer mines, an individual made use of flowing water to sep-

arate gold from the sand. The sand, being much lighter, was washed away. To claim the gold and silver riches in hard rock, miners had to loosen the ore from barren (non ore-bearing) rock. Next they had to crush it into small particles. Only then could they reclaim the precious silver and gold, usually through amalgamation. That process involves using mercury to absorb the yellow metal into a composite, after which the mercury is driven off by heat. Gleaming silver and gold remained.

IN THIS VERY EARLY PHOTOGRAPH of Aurora, taken during a civic event in the mid-1860s, ladies in full skirts are seated on the balcony of the Exchange Hotel.

Hard rock mining took money. It required more than a simple prospector's grubstake. To open and develop a mine required men to use pick and shovel – and sometimes black powder explosive – to probe an ore vein and expose the rich rock. The rock was hauled to a mill by horse-drawn wagons. It took money to "mill" the rock, breaking it down, and still more money to crush it for recovery of the gold and silver.

The ore bodies they worked occurred in branching quartz veins that varied from a fraction of an inch to 80 feet thick, in volcanic rocks. Within weeks at least 14 veins were mapped, consisting mostly of finely granular white quartz.

Mining ventures in the Esmeralda Mining District, as at the more famous Comstock Lode, were financed by capital stock issued through the San Francisco Stock and Exchange Board. Corporate stock rules were different in 1864 than after the establishment of the federal Securities and Exchange Commission in 1913. The difference would play an important role in Aurora's short life.

While corporations were formed and money was raised to begin wresting the riches from Esmeralda's embrace, other enterprising men provided places for the miners to live. Joshua E. Clayton laid out a townsite for Aurora, with streets in a grid. He set aside sites for the courthouse or town hall and other facilities. Quickly, Aurora sprang to life.

The first dwellings in town were dugouts in a steep side of a gulch, covered with canvas tenting. Local rock, laid without mortar, was used to create rough walls. The finest beds in the village were simple straw ticks on rope lattices. Rawhide cots were more common.

In winter the floors were often wet with water that seeped from the hillside. Sourdough starter mix regularly froze through at night.

Twenty-year-old William Hoyt of Placerville, California, was probably typical of the new arrivals in Aurora. He came to town on a Monday in March, 1863, and stayed at the Frémont House. The next day he roamed around the hillsides checking out the mines. By Thursday, with pick in hand, he had a job at a mine. He devoted Sunday to building a cabin. It needed no wiring or plumbing. His new dwelling was presumably just four walls, a door and perhaps a window, and a roof.

A little more than three weeks later he spent time battening the cabin, adding narrow boards over the joints between the wider ones that enclosed the walls. That weekend he made a chimney. It was almost six months before he bought more lumber and put in a floor. When he left Aurora in October, 1864, the cabin was being used as a communal boarding place and so he had to sleep elsewhere.

Aurora's townsite map shows neat, rectangular pattern of streets. The town's central business section developed along Pine Street, paralleling the foot of a steep hillside on the north side of the gully cut through the meadow by the stream. Where the name Aurora came from is unknown. It was applied sometime prior to November 1860. One diarist recorded the *aurora borealis* as having been bright in the night sky above town in July 1861. Perhaps they had seen it from there a year earlier, as well. Another story says one of the three discoverers—Corey, Hicks and Braly—came from Aurora, Ill.

Houses in the struggling mine camp of Monoville, to the west near Mono Lake, were disassembled and loaded in heavy wagons, then reassembled in the flourishing new Esmeralda District. Throughout the long winter months of 1860, settlers arrived with plans to secure their personal fortune. In late spring, 1861, there were 600 people in Aurora.

Aurora is isolated in mountains which are studded with piñon pine, a short-trunked tree full of pitch. There was no timber from which lumber could be cut. Wood building materials, as well as all food, clothing and hardware, were brought in by horse- mule- or ox-drawn wagon. One attribute of Piñon is that it burns with a heat as intense as that of oak or other hardwood. That heat was put to good use in the new town, creating bricks and turning limestone into lime for mortar. As a result, Aurora became a city of brick structures; an impressive fact, but one which would later cause the structures to disappear. piñon also provided firewood to warm the dwellings, an important factor at 7,400 feet above sea level.

When there were only 25 schoolhouses in all of Nevada, just two were built of brick. Aurora boasted of having one of them. It measured 20 by 40 feet, and opened in 1864 with 80 pupils. Aurora was at its peak that year. There were 20 general merchandise stores, a dozen hotels and as many boarding houses, and many, many saloons. The Aurora post office, which opened in September, 1861, was briefly known as "Esmeralda."

After the spring thaw in 1861, Aurora townspeople had been going about building homes and businesses. The mines were gearing up for major production. Far away in Washington, D.C., events were taking place which would have a fascinating – and humorous – effect on the town.

Congress was in pre-Civil War turmoil, arguing over ways to deal with the slavery question in an expanding nation. In the process, Congress on March 2, 1861, created Nevada Territory out of the western part of the existing Utah Territory. In 1849 Congress had approved the state constitution submitted by California. It set the southeastern boundary of the new state as an oblique line from Lake Tahoe (then called Lake

Bigler) southeastward toward the Colorado River.

The enacting legislation provided that Nevada Territory could extend west to the crest of the Sierra – a point somewhat west of the line California had set – *if* California agreed. It did not take long for politicians to perceive that Aurora probably lay somewhere in that controversial zone.

A month later in California, agitation for local government of the Sierra crest led to formation of Mono County. Aurora was designated as the county seat. Residents of the gold camps at Monoville, embryonic Bodie district, and Aurora and vicinity needed a place to record deeds, base a sheriff, and house public records.

President Abraham Lincoln appointed the amiable and capable James W. Nye of New York as territorial governor for the new Nevada Territory. On his arrival in August 1861, Nye set up nine provisional counties and called for an election to select representatives to a Territorial Legislature.

Governor Nye named the southernmost county Esmeralda, and included Aurora in it. Even after the first Territorial Legislature created the county, Nye recognized the difficulty of one town claimed by both a state and a territory. He declined to appoint county officers other than a district attorney and a county surveyor.

The Nevada Territorial governor then personally petitioned the California legislature to relinquish the lands east of the crest of the Sierra. Though polite enough, the Californians were totally unresponsive. A preliminary land survey by his new county surveyor convinced Governor Nye that

Aurora would fall east of the California-Nevada line when formalized. He appointed officers for Esmeralda County, and named Aurora the county seat.

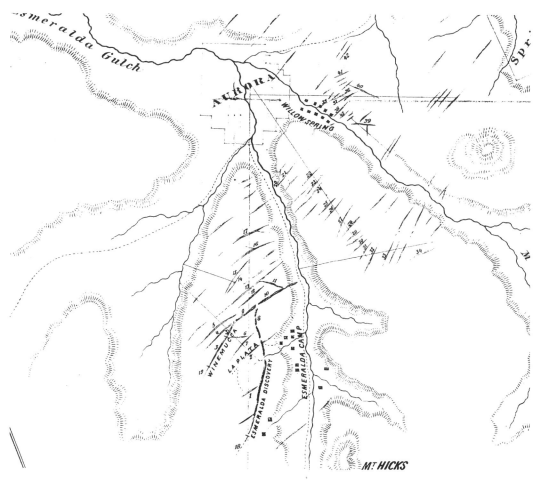

THIS RARE 1862 BRITTON & REY MAP of the Esmeralda District shows the embryonic town of Aurora and claim locations, including the original discovery site. Map scale is 2000 ft. to 1 in.

Aurora was now the county seat for two different counties under two different governments.

On Aug. 31, 1861, the residents of Aurora, Nevada Territory, elected delegates and councilmen to the territory's first legislative session. Four days later, the same voters, as residents of Aurora, California, elected representatives and senators to the California state legislature.

The elections became more lively two years later. By late 1863 there were about 3,000 residents, and more arriving monthly. From the north, surveyors were travelling south, trying to determine the dividing line between California and Nevada. They were not yet close enough to ascertain where Aurora would fall. When election day came, September 2, voters went to the Armory to cast ballots for officers for Esmeralda County, N.T. Amid much humor and joking, they next walked over to the Police Station, and cast votes for officers for Mono County, California.

THE REAL DEL MONTE MILL (left) was sketched in September, 1864, by *Harper's Monthly* correspondent J. Ross Browne. He included the smaller Antelope Mill at right.

It was three weeks later, September 23, before everyone learned for sure that Aurora was three miles within Nevada Territory. The two sheriffs were ready for this: Mono County sheriff-elect H. J. Teel resigned and became deputy sheriff to D. G. Francis in Nevada's Esmeralda County. Had it been determined that California owned Aurora, they had agreed, Francis would have become Teel's deputy.

The other Mono County officers loaded the county records on a wagon and hauled them down to Monoville. Eventually those records found a permanent home in Bridgeport, the present county seat.

Mining and Milling

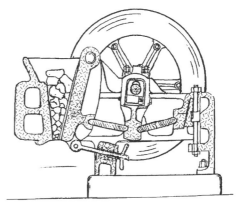

ORE CRUSHER– cross-sectional view. One crusher, with a four-foot flywheel turning at 180 RPM, could break enough quartz to feed 20 stamps. The rough quartz is fed into the hopper at left. As the flywheel turns, the offset piston rises, forcing the right jaw against the fixed left jaw. As the quartz shatters, smaller pieces fall out at the bottom. The handle adjusts the size of the lower opening. Stamp and Crusher drawings are made after W. P. Blake, in Rossiter W. Raymond's *Mines and Mining in the States and Territories*, 1870.

By the summer of 1861, hundreds of mining claims had been staked out on the hills around Aurora. The most productive was to be the Real del Monte strike. It adjoined the Pond Gold and Silver Mining Company claim on the same vein. In those early days of mining law, physical possession was the foundation of Esmeralda mining claim ownership.

As the owners of the Pond and the Real del Monte pushed and pulled along the same vein, disputes ensued. The Pond company settled on a policy which involved both lead and litigation. Reaching into the seamy side of Sacramento, the Pond owners hired men who became known as the Daly gang to secure their claim. Meanwhile, attorneys brought suit in Nevada courts to resolve the ownership clash.

The first mill to crush ore and recover the precious metal was the Pioneer, opened in June 1861. Edmund Green was proprietor. It had eight stamps, six five-foot diameter amalgamating pans and four roasters – it took heat to release gold and silver from the Esmeralda ores. Fabricated in San Francisco, the parts came over the Sierra Nevada in horse-drawn wagons. Total cost was $25,000.

By year's end, the Union Foundry and Coffee Mill had also opened. It had only four stamps and two pans, but boasted a blacksmith and machine shop. Ore treated here was so rich, operators became careless. In 1868, the Coffee Mill was dismantled piece by piece, to recover amalgam from its cracks and crannies.

At the height of production in 1864, Aurora claimed 14 active mills, for a combined total of more than 120 stamps. The first large mill was the Wide West, housed in a 7,440-square-foot building which cost $150,000 to erect, in 1863. It contained 20 stamps and 40 amalgamating pans. Water was fed to

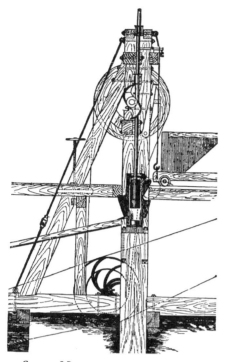

STAMP MILL– cross-sectional view. After being reduced in sized by thhe crusher, ore is fed into the mortar. The 600-pound stamp is lifted by the cog-wheel, then drops onto the ore. When small enough, the ore passes out through grates in the side of the mortar box. It is then ready for amalgamation with mercury.

it from an artesian well. A 600-foot tunnel ran from the mill to the ore ledge. It is hard to equate 1863 dollars to today's dollar; such a building would cost more than 10 times as many dollars today.

The next year, 1864, the Real del Monte Gold and Silver Mining Company mill, situated four miles west on Bodie Creek, eclipsed the Wide West mill. Built of granite and brick at a cost of $250,000, the structure covered 9,600 square feet, all topped by a fine tin roof. It presented a Gothic style of architecture. An adjacent 1,700 square-foot building housed the boilers. A 100-horsepower steam engine powered a pair of 1,700 pound breaking stamps which then fed a 20-stamp battery.

Directly across Bodie Creek was the Antelope Mill, a $150,000 brick structure with an equal number of stamps, but powered by a smaller engine. During 1863, $540,000 in investors' capital built five new mills near Aurora.

As they completed the mills, the rumble of heavy rock breakers reducing quartz boulders, and stamp batteries crushing the ore into workable powder, became an around-the-clock sound in Aurora.

Underground mining in the hard rock of the Esmeralda District made for a long, tiring day. Breaking loose the rich ore involved drilling, blasting, picking, shoveling, and wheeling heavy rock, both ore-bearing and barren, over the rough floor of man-made caverns that drifted from the main shaft, 50 to 100 feet under the surface. To a visitor the timbers placed every few feet appeared like trees in a forest. The smells were of dust and cold rock and sweating men. The sound of the drill and hammer was heard. Candles threw a dim light which glistened on shirtless laborers.

One Aurora resident who tried working as a mill hand and then attempted to mine for ore was Samuel Langhorn Clemens. A Missourian, Sam came

West with his brother, Orion Clemens, whom Lincoln had selected as Nevada's number two appointed official, its territorial secretary. Footloose and fancy free, Sam had a circle of friends that made his life in Aurora enjoyable. Though money was scarce, he maintained a free-spending image. He collected from Aurora trash piles the refuse of the wealthy – empty tin cans that had held fine food, and champagne bottles – and used them as litter in his own front yard.

Sam spent some of his evenings writing articles about Aurora for the Virginia City *Territorial Enterprise*. Eventually he gave up mining to become a reporter for the *Enterprise*. In Virginia City he adopted the pen name "Mark Twain." A few years later he immortalized his Aurora days in the still-popular book *Roughing It*.

INTERVIEWING the Wide West mine, from *Roughing It*.

The 1860s workday was long. Men toiled from before dawn to a late dinnertime. Many of the mills operated around the clock, seven days a week. There was no radio or movie house. Indeed, there was no electricity. Aurora's population consisted largely of hardy young men. After the workday was through, they still had energy to burn, so they created fun. It took all forms.

One was the arrival of the mail, every other evening. Sometime between 10 and 11 p.m. someone would hear the sound of the stage rumbling over the hills. A cry would go up: "Stage comin'." By the time the vehicle came to a stop, a crowd of eager miners surrounded it. In a few minutes the crowd was at the doors of the adjacent Express and Post offices. The Express office had a shipping list of the incoming packages and envelopes. Recipients could claim them immediately. The Post Office clerk distributed the box mail promptly on its arrival. The general delivery crowd had to wait until 8 a.m. to receive their missives of business, family or love. Since Aurora's winters were hard to endure, many of its residents left town in October and November. Then they returned in March, after wintering in San Francisco, Sacramento, or other milder climes. Each spring newcomers, seeking to find their own mine, or to find employment in the many mines and mills already there, joined the returnees. For those who remained, the winter months were long and full of difficulties. Mountain roads were nearly impassable after being cut up by wagon and stage wheels, and then frozen. Mail arrived by muleback, or was carried in by men on skis. Bitter cold nights left food and water frozen in the uninsulated brick and stone homes.

From time to time there were crisp, clear winter Sundays. Miles away, deep snow on the prominent peaks of Mounts Corey, Braly and Hicks stood out in sharp detail against cloudless blue skies. Parties of ladies and gents went sleigh riding. Others sledded the nearby slopes or traversed them on long wooden skies.

For Christmas Day, Aurorans decorated a hall with pine boughs and one or more community Christmas trees. Everyone brought presents. Gifts loaded down the trees and heavier articles were laid under them. "Santa" arrived to hand the packages around. About a hundred children celebrated on one happy Christmas Eve. There were appropriate recitations and singing and joy.

On the first of May, 1862, the hills echoed laughter and conversation from a May Day picnic. On a hillside near the town "cozy arbors were fitted up with seats and carpets to cover the sand." Boxes, baskets, bottles, cans and more provided food to be laid out on a white tablecloth. Miss Hattie Green was crowned Queen of May, and she recited a poem "To The American Flag." Accompanied by a guitar, Mrs. Garesche sang "Charming May." In the evening the gathering retired to a grand ball. Lt. Herman Noble, U.S. Army, was a big hit in epaulets, stripes and brass buttons.

Three months later, the Rev. Charles Yager presided over the first wedding in town. G. W. Smith, 30, married Caroline N. Parker, 16. Although predominantly a town of men, there were numerous other ladies in town. Mrs. Hutchinson, a leader among the married women, organized a Sewing Circle.

Births were not recorded as they are today, and no official records have survived of the new arrivals. Death often recorded its presence through probate bonds; the first remembered A. S. Kent, who died in September 1861. By September 1863, 70 burials had occurred in the Aurora cemetery – 53 by natural death, and the other 17 by violence, or otherwise.

Mining Camp Days

Many of Aurora's single men lived in boarding houses, or took their meals there. A week's board at any of several dining rooms was less than $10. Sunday mornings, for variety, J. Marchant's bakery offered Boston Brown Bread and Beans.

Visitors to town were drafted as speakers. Typical was the noted *Harpers Magazine* writer J. Ross Browne, who arrived in September 1864. A group invited him to speak, and Browne agreed to do so to benefit the Sanitary Fund, the Civil War equivalent of the Red Cross. More than 170 people attended, paying 50¢ each, to hear "a conversational narrative of the principal incidents of his varied and interesting career." A week later he returned to Preble & Devoe's Hall to tell a full house about "The Peculiar Customs of the People of Germany."

The Sanitary Fund benefitted from most of the events held in Aurora during the war years. The fund was created in 1863. One gift to the fund from Aurora was two silver bars, each valued at more than $2,250.

James Stark, a famed East Coast tragedian, arrived in Nevada Territory to perform in Virginia City. He visited Aurora with Governor Nye, and promptly invested in the Esmeralda mines. When he became a resident to manage his business interests, friends prevailed on him to entertain in Aurora. On one

such occasion, he delivered ten readings and recitations to benefit the Deluge Bucket Co. No. 1. With music between selections, he recited several old favorites, with titles like "Young Lochinvar," to a full house.

Aurora had its own Brass Band. Its members gave concerts on Sunday afternoons. They played when the volunteer firefighters of Engine Company No. 1 held a Grand Ball. The new pumper truck had arrived, providing an excuse for the party. Members of the other fire unit, Deluge Bucket Company No. 1, joined the celebration. Most of the men present wore uniforms – band members, firemen, and militia members.

A few weeks later the engine company held a parade to honor Mrs. Hutchinson's Sewing Circle. The ladies had raised funds to equip the hose wagon with canvas fire hose.

Charles Cardinell taught ballroom dancing Tuesday and Thursday evenings at his Academy. There were several well-attended churches in town. Saloons were open all night.

Parades, necessarily held in the evening after work, always drew a crowd. One big parade celebrated proclamation of Nevada statehood. It was a grand event, held the night before Election Day. Heavy paper was imprinted with mottos and slogans. These were mounted on a four-sided framework with a lantern inside, all atop a single pole. Individual paraders carried these "flaming transparencies" which were easily read despite the dark. Larger canvas paintings and signs were mounted on wagons, and similarly backlighted. Other paraders carried torches. One editor noted "The long line of fire that lit up the heavens was sublimely beautiful." Candles in every window of a hundred homes added a "grand illumination" aspect to parades. Six inches of fresh snow enhanced the lighting.

Union sentiment ran high, and the voter turnout the next day reflected great support for Abraham Lincoln. A. S. Peck of Aurora was elected as one of three Nevada delegates to the electoral college. In the national tally, Aurora's pro-Lincoln vote did not count – Mr. Peck became ill and died before he could cast his electoral vote.

At the height of the mining boom, Aurorans supported two daily newspa-

IN 1863, San Francisco publisher Warren Holt's map of Nevada showed Aurora to be within California.

BY 1866, Holt's cartographers had placed Aurora safely within Nevada.

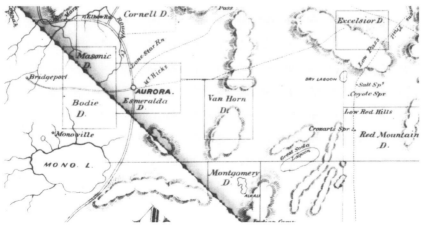

AURORA'S PROMINENT Exchange Hotel, as pictured in *Thompson & West's History of Nevada, 1881.*

pers, the *Esmeralda Union* and the Aurora *Daily Times.* American newspaper editors of the day were outspoken in all matters, and Aurora's were no different. On more than one occasion, Aurora readers took comment personally, and called the editor to account. E. A. Sherman, editor of the *Esmeralda Union,* praised the election defeat of a "people's ticket." He said it had been supported by "every ruffian and Jeff Davis brawler in town." The next evening, he was confronted by several supporters of that particular political crew. Sherman suffered a bloody nose before he was rescued by friends.

Like any village of note, Aurora had a town characters. One was known only as "Vincent." He continually wandered the streets of Aurora, and was assumed to be crazy. In the spring of 1864 the county commissioners drew $50 for Vincent's assistance.

When a mining accident blinded Isaac Davis, the town rallied to his support. Davis became well known, benefits were held for him, and for several years, friends looked to his welfare.

Civil War patriotism gave rise to strong political clubs that met regularly. The largest and strongest in Aurora was the Union Club, an organization with a distinct Republican bent.

Fire in Aurora

Structure fires were a fact of life in mid 19th century towns. In those days before electricity, lanterns and candles provided light after sundown. Even restaurants cooked food on woodburning kitchen stoves. Stoves and fireplaces provided heat. A mistake in handling flames could be disastrous.

Aurora's firefighting consisted of one volunteer bucket brigade and one pumper wagon. Volunteers manned the pumphandles on either side of the wagon. The force with which they raised and lowered the handles, or brakes, regulated the pressure.

Aurora had its share of small fires, and escaped a major one until early one cold morning in January 1866. The weather had been clear for ten days past, but rather cold, thermometer ranging from six degrees to twelve degrees above zero every night. On the seventh, after the fire had burned its course, the Aurora correspondent of the Sacramento *Daily Union* told readers of the loss:

> Yesterday morning we had a more destructive fire than all others heretofore in the town of Aurora. It broke out between two and three o'clock in the morning, in a frame building that had not been occupied for a year past. The wind was blowing fiercely at the time and the fire spread with great rapidity, burning all the frame buildings on both sides of Antelope Street, between Pine and Aurora, including the stores of Carland & Co., and F. Hafky. The former saved most of his goods, though in a damaged state, by a vault in the rear of his store. The latter lost all his goods, furniture and everything. His loss is very much deplored by the citizens....Had it not have been for the almost superhuman efforts of the citizens and firemen the whole town would have been in ashes. The fire is supposed to have been the work of an incendiary.
>
> During the day a snowstorm set in and snow fell to the depth of about three inches.

Military and Indians

One war-spawned activity which caused great civic pride was Aurora's militia units. There were two of them – The Aurora City Guard, under Captain J. W. Palmer, and The Esmeralda Rangers under Captain H. J. Teel. The Rangers were established as a cavalry unit. When they could not obtain carbines, they shifted to an infantry unit. Aurorans felt a patriotic pride as they watched the Rangers return from a summer evening drill. They marched home to the music of the fife and drum, their new Minie rifles reflecting moonlight.

For those accepting a full-time enlistment, Captain J. W. Calder was recruiting Company F, Nevada Volunteers, U.S. Cavalry, in Aurora. By March of 1864 he had 88 enlistees.

The U.S. Army set up a camp near town, popularly called Camp Noble in honor of the lieutenant in command. Lt. Noble and 50 men with muskets from the 2d Cavalry, California Volunteers, had been dispatched from Ft. Churchill to quell an Indian uprising in nearby Owens Valley.

The Native Americans of the region were Paiutes, whose homeland centered north and east, on the Walker River and Lake. Some of them provided domestic support to the Aurora area. They brought in firewood and often provided wild currents, or fresh Brook Trout, in exchange for money or food.

Occasionally the Indians provided entertainment. One Sunday afternoon the local Paiutes had a feast dance in town to amuse the citizens. Onlookers gave them coins. As 20 to 30 Indians formed a circle, they began a humming nasal tune, stamping first one foot then the other, and shaking their arms. They had paint on their faces and backs. Their bodies were naked except for a crude skirt around their loins.

Other Indians resisted the invasion of their native lands. The group living southwest of Aurora, at Owens River, especially resented the influx of the men raising livestock to provide meat for the region. In early 1862 they rose up in reaction to the situation.

The winter of 1861-62 was severe. Cattle grazed Indian hunting grounds, forcing out the deer. There was a poor harvest of piñon pine nuts, a main staple of the Indians. The Indians killed settlers' cattle for food, and settlers responded by shooting Indians. In retaliation the Indians killed several white men.

Aurora, as the nearest town, became a focus for reports on the "excitement." A public meeting on the Indian troubles was held on March 12. Following that John J. Kellogg led a group of 18 men to aid the settlers.

The inhabitants of the Owens River area were all cattlemen. They now "forted up" at Independence Creek, 30 miles above Owens Lake. The 18 men from Aurora arrived in relief of the graziers, who took the field 60 strong. "Col." William Mayfield served as leader. That day they had a skirmish in force with the Indians. Cage J. Pleasant of Aurora was killed outright and Harrison Morrison of Visalia was mortally wounded.

The Indians pursued Mayfield's force, which took shelter in a ditch the Indians had dug to irrigate native plants. There, while lighting his pipe, Sheriff N. F. Scott of Aurora, Mono County, was killed by an Indian sniper.

That night Mayfield's company escaped and returned to the protected camp, abandoning their ammunition supply and 18 horses, and leaving their dead on the field.

On the march, they met Lt. Col. George Evans with two lieutenants and 40 men of the 2d Cavalry, California Volunteers, from Los Angeles. They joined forces and again pursued the Indians.

In the meantime Governor Nye learned of the difficulty on Owens River from Indian Agent Warren Wasson. Wasson requested enough troops to put down the disturbance, and prevent the war from spreading to the Walker River and Pyramid Lake Paiutes. General George Wright, commander of the Department of the Pacific, ordered Captain E. A. Rowe of the 2d Cavalry California Volunteers, stationed at Fort Churchill, to send 50 men to the scene.

Captain Rowe put Lieutenant Noble in command of the detachment. Rowe told Noble not to engage the Indians without the sanction of Wasson. The Indian agent had hoped to meet with the Indians and end the tension through a parlay. When Lieutenant Noble met Col. Evans on April 7, Evans assumed overall command and ordered the unit to join in the pursuit of the Indians. Wasson became a spectator.

On the second day, Colonel Evans, suspecting the Indians were hiding in a canyon, sent Sergeant Gillespie and nine men to reconnoiter in advance of the main command. Indians fired and rained arrows on the squad almost as soon as it entered the canyon. Sergeant Gillespie was killed and a corporal was wounded. Evans ordered an attack, with the cavalry under Evans moving to take the slope on the right of the defile. Meanwhile Lieutenant Noble, with

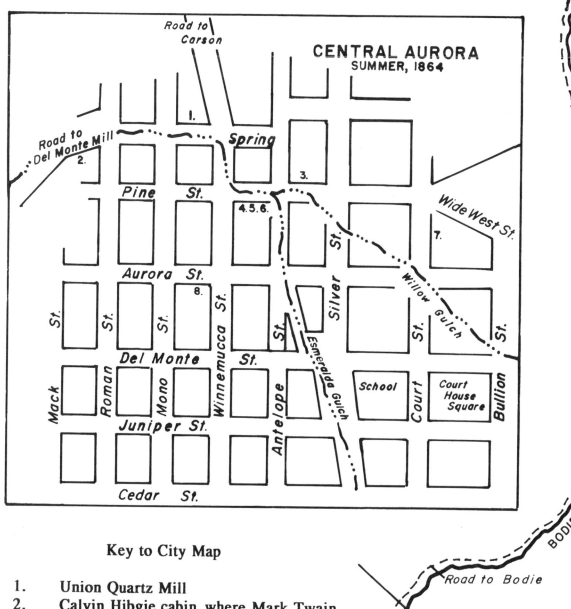

Key to City Map

1.   Union Quartz Mill
2.   Calvin Hibgie cabin, where Mark Twain
       lived in 1862
3.   Wingate's Hall
4.   Fleischman & Kaufman general merchandise
5.   Howard & Sanchez Bank
6.   Levy Brothers general merchandise store
7.   Duane Hose Company fire station
8.   Home of Mayor and Mrs. Ramon B. Sanchez

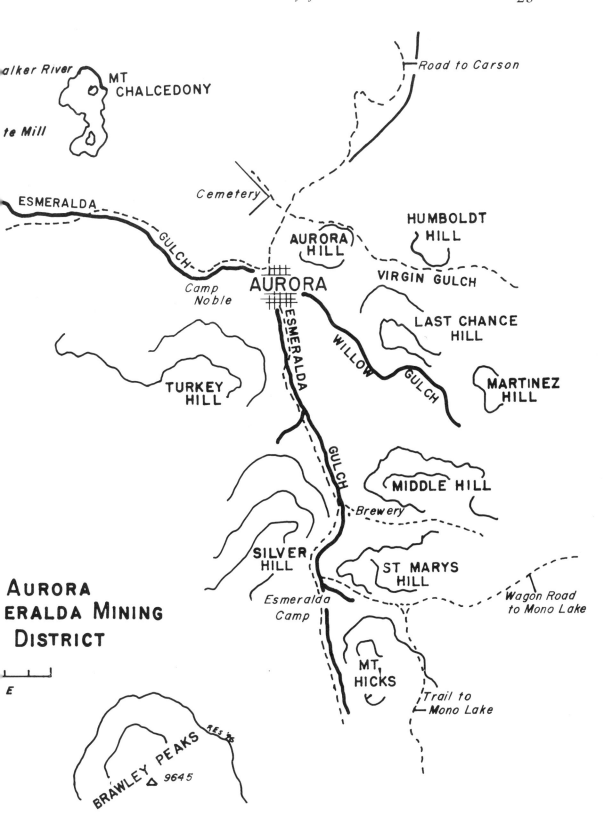

alker River

MT CHALCEDONY

te Mill

Road to Carson

Cemetery

ESMERALDA

GULCH

Camp Noble

HUMBOLDT HILL

AURORA HILL

VIRGIN GULCH

AURORA

ESMERALDA

WILLOW GULCH

LAST CHANCE HILL

MARTINEZ HILL

TURKEY HILL

GULCH

MIDDLE HILL

Brewery

SILVER HILL

ST MARYS HILL

Wagon Road to Mono Lake

Esmeralda Camp

AURORA
ERALDA MINING
DISTRICT

E

MT HICKS

Trail to Mono Lake

BRAWLEY PEAKS
9645

his company and a few citizens, mounted the heights on the left. The other troops remained below, in reserve. Under fire, Noble succeeded in gaining his assigned position. Mayfield died during the assault.

Unable to engage the Indians in open combat, Noble withdrew. Colonel Evans' men had left their home station with limited field provisions. As these were now running low, he and his troops departed for Los Angeles. Lieutenant Noble then escorted the Owens Valley ranchers, with 4,000 cattle and 2,500 sheep, to pastures in Nevada. The Owens Valley conflict continued sporadically for several years.

The Civil War Touches Aurora

In Aurora, on a cold but sunny March 4, 1865, the citizens paused to observe the day President Lincoln took the oath of office for his second term. They raised flags throughout the town and celebrated happily.

A few weeks later the surrender of General Lee's army brought an even greater celebration. As word came in by telegraph, flags were raised, guns fired and black powder exploded. The town went wild with enthusiasm and joy. The telegraph operator, George Senf, known simply as "Graph," was bearer of the great tidings. He was glad-handed by everyone. The general celebration lasted through the night.

Too few days later, news arrived of a tragic event. It fell on Graph to relay word of the assassination of President Lincoln. Businessmen draped their stores in black. Mining activity as well as commerce shut down. A large procession was held and public funeral addresses were given by two prominent residents, Dr. B. S. Mason and M. T. Gough.

The major battles of the Civil War occurred far away from Nevada and California. There was, nevertheless, a very real threat the Civil War could reach the West. As late as February 1864, James Snedden, Secretary of War for the Confederate States, sent instructions to recruit troops in California. He was to drill them in Arizona. The goal was to annex the southern half of California through military action.

General Wright, at the Presidio, kept himself informed on secessionist activities. In Nevada, Colonel P. Edward Connor, commanding military forces in the Territory, issued an order forbidding the utterance of traitorous sentiments. His order forbade public demonstrations favoring secession. In August 1862, Lieutenant Noble was recuperating in Aurora after he had become ill during the Owens River campaign. He was insulted repeatedly by hoots and cheers for Jefferson Davis. In mid-month, a band of "rebels" held a rally, cheering Davis, Stonewall Jackson and the Southern Confederacy. With Lieutenant Noble in command, a detail of ten members of the Esmeralda Rifles arrested a leading Confederacy supporter, Augustus Quinton.

Under Wright's and Connor's orders, Quinton faced a choice: he could take an oath of allegiance, or be sent to Fort Churchill. There he would be forced to spend 10 hours a day marching around the sun-drenched parade ground, under guard, with a 60-pound pack of sand on his back. Quinton chose to take the oath.

Confederate sympathizers created minor disturbances in Aurora. More serious, often deadly, acts came from another cause. The town continued to endure the Daly Gang, brought in to protect the Pond Company's mining interests. The gang held the claims by force, while the owners battled the competing Real del Monte Mine owners in court. There was an unsteady flow of shootings and other violence, usually traceable to the Daly Gang. One body was dumped in an ore mill's slime pond. Beatings and general rowdiness were common, and in the town's first three years there were more than two dozen violent deaths.

The jury reached its verdict in the Pond versus Real del Monte lawsuit in December 1863. The Pond lost. Its mining claims were turned over to the Real del Monte company, and the Daly Gang "security force" was dismissed. Though unemployed, they did not leave town.

On February 1, 1864, Daly and companions killed an upstanding citizen in revenge for an earlier incident. The townspeople rose up in reaction.

A Vigilance Committee formed, and within two weeks it hanged Daly and three of his followers. The Committee ordered other gang members out of town. Throughout the days of the incident, the telegraph kept Governor Nye informed. A few days after the hanging, he arrived in Aurora to insure peaceable law and order. With the governor was Territorial Provost Marshal Jacob VanBokkelyn of Virginia City, who had been "chief of police" for San Francisco's Committee of Vigilance in 1856.

As the Sacramento *Daily Union* noted, they were welcomed by the people, but too late for any effect.

The Aurora Committee of Vigilance disbanded. An entry in the ledger from A. M. Wingate's general store suggests one of the last committee purchases was a small cask of brandy, perhaps bought for a final celebration of their "success."

Aurorans again turned their attention to mining. To their dismay they were learning there was no rich ore below a depth of about 100 feet. Shortly after Governor Nye left, following a three-day stay, a committee of Real del Monte stockholders arrived. Accompanying them was the firm's president. The Real del Monte, like the Wide West mine, had reached below the 100-foot level. Ore bodies were pinching out. A breakdown of Real del Monte mill equipment further reduced the shipments of bullion from Aurora. After other problems with the operation came to light, the Real del Monte superintendent in Aurora was fired.

A few days later the stockholders committee announced its finding of numerous irregularities in Real del Monte management. It became clear that stock prices had been subjected to insider trading. The same was true of many Comstock mines, since the lack of stock market regulation allowed manipulation of prices. All this – Comstock and Esmeralda inconsistencies combined – undermined public confidence in mining stocks. There was needed only a light push to bring it down, and that was furnished from Aurora by the stockholders' committee report.

The San Francisco stock market of the 1860s dealt almost exclusively with mining issues. The resultant crash there of Real del Monte stock prices caused many failures among the brokers of San Francisco. The remaining brokers never again held Aurora in favor.

The capital stock for mining companies was "assessable." That meant that, unlike today, the company could tell its stockholders it needed more money, and call for them to pay their share of the added amount. Rumors were common that a particular assessment was to pay officers' salaries, or some other abuse of the system. The assessments could be burdensome. Those who did not pay stood to forfeit their entire investment. Many frustrated stockholders resisted paying, and the legal notice columns of late 1864 and through 1865 carried long lists of forfeitures.

While it lasted, Aurora's gold and silver ore was indeed rich. Mills only worked ore with mineral values of $75 or more to the ton. Gold- and silver-bearing quartz was limited to a band from 50 to 100 feet below the surface, and most mines had reached that depth. After the stock crash of 1864, a long, slow decline began in Aurora. Production continued, at a reduced volume, through the balance of the 1860s.

There was another reason 1864 became both the high point and the low. The tide had turned in the Civil War. With the outlook for peace the price of silver declined rapidly. Nevada's mines were opened at the outset of the war. At the same time, Eastern factories turned to war production. By the end of the war in 1865, California, of necessity, had become self sufficient. Nevada mines had helped provide the impetus of California's transformation by financing much of the change.

Aurora gold and silver production during the 1860s has been estimated at about $30 million in bullion. Stated in a modern price for gold, it was somewhat more than $300 million. By comparison, the Belcher Mine on the Comstock Lode at Virginia City alone produced $16.7 million in bullion during one three-year period, 1871-1873.

As the mines faded, owners dismantled their cabins and hauled them up-canyon to the rapidly expanding village of Bodie. One means for survival of Aurora's remaining miners was to combine various mineral claims. When mines were combined, the number of men employed was reduced, and the town shrank in response.

To carry themselves through this dry spell, many individuals became "coasters," miners who sought out overlooked individual boulders still containing rich ore. There were enough of these rocks around to keep a few mills in operation.

Court and recorder service for the active mining camps of Candelaria and Columbus in the eastern part of Esmeralda County provided enough legal business to keep the county seat in Aurora.

In 1871, *Atlantic Monthly* began carrying a series by a 29-year-old geologist named Clarence King, called "Mountaineering in the Sierra Nevada." King drew immediate interest and widespread fame.

In the course of his research for the articles, King visited Aurora. He sensationalized the town in the series, for all the nation to read, as a murderous city past its prime:

> Alas for Aurora once so active and bustling with silver mines and its almost daily murder. . . . Now her sad streets are lined with closed doors . . . A painful silence broods over quartz mills, and through the whole deserted town one perceives that melancholy. . . . The "boys" have gone off to merrily shoot one another somewhere else, leaving poor Aurora in the hands of a sort of coroner's jury who gather nightly at the one saloon and hold dreary inquests over departed enterprise.

Aurorans felt greatly insulted. When King returned the next year on a U.S. Geological Survey team, the offended residents gave him a subtle snub. On this second visit, King was accompanied by the prominent artist Albert Bierstadt, then enjoying fame for his dramatic Sierra mountain paintings. The Aurora correspondent never mentioned King by name, and instead told Sacramento *Daily Union* readers only that a *nameless*

> . . . party of United States Government geological surveyors have been in this vicinity for several days past, taking observations of the mountains and country generally, but I can give you nothing definite as to the result. Bierstadt is with them, taking views for his private use.

During the 1870s the idea of a deep shaft developed. Town boosters convinced themselves that the barren rock at the 100-foot depth was simply a cap over richer ore deep below. They dreamed of a 1,000 foot shaft. H. M. Yerington of the Virginia & Truckee Railroad organized the New Real del Monte company in late 1877 to pursue that dream. The company opened with a five million dollar capital fund.

Work began on December 5, 1877, under supervision of George Daly (no relation to the Daly gang). The site was, appropriately perhaps, Last Chance Hill. There were three parts to the shaft, two for hoisting and one for a pump. The first station, or underground platform, was established 300 feet down, where a quartz vein looked promising. Work proceeded in three shifts, around the clock.

Down they went. At 500 feet a heavy flow of water began flooding the shaft. That had been anticipated, and the shaft compartment was in place for drain lines. They brought in the largest water pump obtainable on the West Coast. Still hopeful, they continued down through the barren quartz.

Probing down the first 800 feet took until 1881. Then came a day when the pump no longer seemed capable of keeping up with inflow. Superintendent Daly nearly lost his life when he rode down in the cage to assess the problem. Descending, the cage continued down into water, threatening the passengers with drowning. Above ground an alert engineer saw slight slackness in the cables, and quickly drew the cage back up.

They stopped at the next level up. Miners and equipment were hastily loaded, leaving behind the ore car, tracks and excess equipment. The cage was raised to the surface, and the deep probe venture ended. The water level eventually stabilized at 300 feet.

After that, even the town boosters lost faith. Within a short time only the hardiest of believers remained. Despite the declining population, Aurora managed to keep its status as the seat of Esmeralda County government until 1883. Then Hawthorne, a growing town on the Carson & Colorado Railroad (another H. M. Yerington project), took over county leadership.

The Aurora lodge of the Free and Accepted Masons remained active until 1888, when membership dwindled to five. In 1863 the first Worshipful Master, James Stark, presented the lodge with a set of officers' jewels, set in Aurora silver. In 1888 the jewels were sold to the new lodge in Lovelock. A carpet with the Masonic emblem was sent to the Reno lodge, and the charter was surrendered. Aurora's post office was discontinued in May, 1897.

AS AURORA DECLINED at the close of the 19th Century, both homes and business structures were abandoned. Aurora's brick buildings remained, awaiting the next mining boom.

LOOKING DOWN AND SOUTHEASTERLY from the cliff to the west of Aurora, a photographer in 1890 recorded the remaining structures of this gold mining camp of the 1860s and 70s. During those years Aurora was an incorporated city for less than two years, beginning in March, 1863. Mayor Sanchez's home is the two-story brick in the lower right portion of the above photograph. High above the townsite at top right, are the mine buildings which housed the Del Monte Mine hoistworks, whose mill was situated on Bodie Creek, five miles to the west. A contemporary sketch of the mill is shown on page 12.

FROM A SIMILAR VANTAGE POINT in 1995, the once great town of Aurora is reduced to foundations and rubble, with not one of the sturdy brick buildings left intact.

Aurora's Twentieth Century Mining Boom

Esmeralda's story was not over yet. Aurora was to have one more chance as a town.

Discovery of rich silver ore at Tonopah in 1900, and rich finds at Goldfield in 1902, led mining-conscious individuals to try to revive Aurora. New, more efficient mining and milling techniques were now available. In the early years miners cast aside all but the richest of rock. The crude mill processes had left gold and silver in tailings which new methods could recover.

In 1905 J. S. Cain and associates acquired 46 of the significant claims in Esmeralda district. In November a weekly newspaper, the Aurora *Borealis,* began publication, although it survived for less than ten months.

The following year Cain put a 20-stamp mill in operation. When the workmen arrived, enough people were living in Aurora to justify reopening a post office. The old Aurora Emporium building of the Levy brothers was bought

outright for that purpose. The buyers sent a check for $250 to the Levys, and the key and title came by return mail.

The Emporium was housed in a large brick building with a full basement. It had no windows in one side wall and none in the back wall. On the other two walls, facing Pine and Antelope streets, big iron fire-shutters were securely locked over the old doors.

The new owners opened the front door. They stepped inside. As their eyes adjusted to the dim light in the long-dark building, they saw an astounding sight. Here was a well-stocked general merchandise business, arrested in time decades earlier! The last Levy brother had left behind the full inventory of goods.

Miners' clothing and woolen underwear, buggy whips and segars – it was all there. In the manner of merchandising then in effect, lanterns, water buckets, tea kettles and lunch buckets hung from ceiling hooks. A coil of fine manila rope inside the door was worth the cost of the entire building.

As if the upstairs goods were not enough, the basement also held real trea-

THE TWENTIETH CENTURY rejuvenation of Aurora meant that many businesses were reopened, most of which were housed in existing structures.

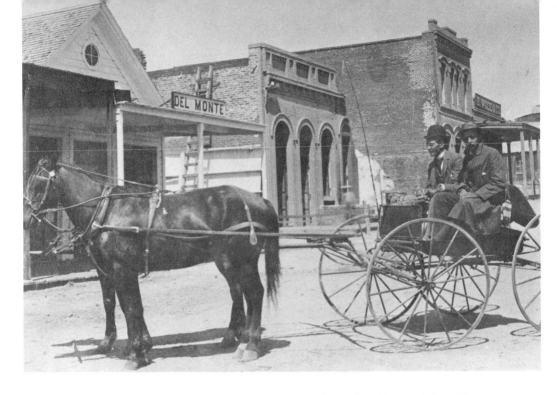

MINING EXPERTS SET TO LEAVE Aurora after visiting the Real Del Monte Mine, The Esmeralda District's longest-lived mining operation.

sure. Barrels of fine whiskey had quietly aged to smoothness. Champagne remained wrapped in the straw in which it had been shipped from France. Untouched liquors, brandies, and wines waited for a buyer.

Paiutes in the region were soon resplendent in Prince Albert dress suits. Marked to be sold for $65 each, they were now dispensed at just $1. A ready market was found among the local Indians.

The Cain mining effort continued until late 1912, when W. Lester Mangum bought it out for $200,000. Two months later, Mangum diluted his interest, taking on Jesse Knight and three others as partners. They built a 500-ton-per-day mill, with Mangum as general manager.

In June 1914, the sound of ore crushing once more rumbled through the venerable

Esmeralda Mining District. The one mill of 1914 could produce nearly as much crushed ore as all the old mills combined.

The ghosts of old Aurora must have been hopeful that their town would once again thrive. That was not to be.

It shocked Knight, who came from Provo, Utah, to see the saloons, and even a brothel, set up shop in the old buildings remaining in Aurora. He promptly established a new town over the hill, naming it Mangum. Although the post office remained at Aurora, most of the miner's residences were now some distance away.

The town of saloons and similar other businesses did begin to rustle anew, but the reprise was short-lived.

Tonopah and Goldfield were booming. Their mine owners had money to invest. Goldfield Consolidated Mines Company bought out the Mangum-Knight consortium. By 1915 Reno banker George Wingfield was presiding over a Goldfield Consolidated subsidiary named Aurora Consolidated Mines. This effort continued for three years, always at a loss.

Aurora Consolidated worked over the mines and the old mill tailings. It processed more than 633 thousand tons of ore, and extracted nearly $1,850,000 in gold and silver. The nation had gone to war, and the cost of labor had become high. Profits were marginal. Goldfield Consolidated decided to close down its Aurora operation.

Workers dismantled the mill and took it and other buildings to the home operation in Goldfield. The company town of Mangum disappeared. The old buildings of old Aurora were once again abandoned.

Mining techniques had undergone great change. No future mining operation would be as labor intensive as those of the 1860s, or even of the 1910s. When significant mining returned to the district several decades later, no nearby town was needed for the few workers. They could commute from more inviting locales.

During the long years of decline the wooden structures that had not been dismantled and hauled away were stripped to become firewood for the remaining residents. Beams were salvaged for timbering in shafts and tunnels. Finally only the brick structures remained.

When the Esmeralda mines were booming, lumber and hardware had to be brought in by the wagonload. Freight costs made it expensive. Clay, limestone, and hot-burning piñon pine were plentiful. Industrious Aurorans had molded clay, stacked it into self-contained kilns, and created a quality brick.

AURORA WAS FESTIVE during national holidays, with flags, bunting and other patriotic decorations much in evidence.

In other kilns, limestone was heated to create lime. Mixed with sand, it made a mortar to bind bricks into walls and structures.

Unlike cement-based mortar, lime leaches out of the joints over time. It loses its etched grip on the brick and sand. With little effort these bricks can be cleaned of mortar remnants, and reused.

This doomed the Aurora buildings, which had withstood the effects of time for nearly a century. When a building boom exploded in Reno and especially in Southern California immediately after World War II, Aurora was looted for its brick. The buildings were dismantled and the brick was recycled to become "used brick" homes in sprawling new suburbs.

The very substance of the city became the reason the ghost town was razed.

Epilogue

Little evidence remains of Aurora's prime years. Sagebrush and native grasses have reclaimed the mountain park that once rang with the sounds of a mining camp. The leisurely visitor can stroll down from St. John's Cemetery to the top of the cliff which overlooks the village site from the West. From that vantage point the streets of the town can be distinguished. On the far hillsides are waste dumps from Aurora's once-rich mines.

Some days, when a visitor stands there looking out over the vale, a golden eagle will be hunting the old townsite, soaring below the viewer with its haunting cry.

Aurora has faded into history.

AN OVERSHOT WATER WHEEL powered this Aurora mill, shown in ruins about 1910.

Aurora's Cemetery

On the hilltop north of Aurora lies the city's old burying ground. On the town map created in 1863, it was designated "St. John's Cemetery." Stretching across the hilltop, the cemetery is still in use; thoughtful friends from Hawthorne see to its maintenance.

The contemporary newspapers chronicle many deaths in early Aurora, by violence, by accident and from natural causes. Burial began here as quickly as the town came to life. While some caskets may have been re-interred later, closer to their native home, most were probably marked with wooden headboards which have disappeared. Less than fifty identifiable headstones remain. The earliest is that of William E. Carder, a stone memorial erected by the anguished wife of a violent man who died a violent death in 1864.

Among the largest memorials remaining is that of W. M. Boring. He was a pioneer in Aurora who served in the Nevada State Senate in 1871, and died the following year. The obelisk at his gravesite was crafted of stone from the Nevada State Prison quarry in Carson City.

Many remaining stones clearly convey poignant reminders of the harshness of life at this frontier town.; In 1868 E.F. Fredericks buried his wife, and beside her, two weeks later, buried his newborn daughter. At another site rest the children of Horace (Hoddie) and Lizzie Marden: Daisy, four; Pearl, two; Frank, eight; and Dick, six. All four died within a ten-day period in February 1878. Their firstborn, James, died at the age of seven in March 1865. Hoddie is buried nearby.

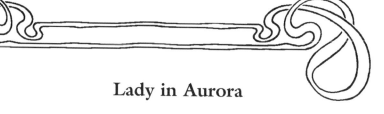

Lady in Aurora

Horses' hooves and iron-rimmed wagon wheels constantly churned the unpaved streets of Aurora. Dust rose to make the air of the city hazy. Dust hung above the streets when the wind was still. Dust infiltrated the tightest of houses when the wind blew, settling on floors, furniture and furnishings.

It took a rain shower to settle the dust and clear the air. Only then could Laura and her husband Ramon Sanchez enjoy a walk around the booming new town.

Ramon Sanchez brought his new wife Laura to Aurora in 1862. Their luggage accompanied them, tied on top of the stagecoach. When they arrived she was dismayed to find three jars of pomade broke in Laura's trunk during the trip over the Sierra Nevada. The oily hair dressing soiled all of her skirts, and her new calico dress. For the first few days she had only her traveling dress for mornings, and a walking dress for evenings.

Aurora was a new town when she arrived. Lumber, cut that spring in the mountains around Big Meadows, was quickly nailed up to create houses for the booming village.

Wide cracks soon developed in their newly-built home as the fresh-cut lumber shrank. Cold mountain winds blew up through the kitchen floor, chilling feet and delivering more of the ever-present dust. The carpeting available in Aurora stores in 1862 was flimsy, so Laura covered the floors in most rooms with a more durable – and less expensive – matting. The little house required a daily sweeping. Laura spent an hour each week just dusting her trinket shelf.

Ramon Sanchez was a partner in the banking house of Howard and Sanchez. The firm was associated with William Ralston's prestigious Donohoe & Ralston Bank in San Francisco. During 1864 Mr. Sanchez served as mayor of Aurora. In letters, his wife always called him "Mr. Sanchez," or "Mr. S." In one letter to her sister she referred to him as "my lord and master."

Laura's family moved to California when she was young, and prospered. The neighbors considered her a "city lady" from a wealthy family in San Francisco. As a result, curiosity often drew local women to visit. Most times Laura found it a bother. But her family had come from Kentucky and she was well trained as a Southern lady, so she returned each visit.

Though the slab walls and floor of her kitchen made the room drafty, she enjoyed cooking in it. She was proud of the kitchen's neat, shiny appearance. Laura said it was impossible to imagine that anything prepared there would not be splendid.

Mr. and Mrs. Sanchez regularly entertained guests in their home. Local businessmen, and friends from California who came up for a look at the mines, often came to dinner. On one especially memorable day the Episcopal Bishop for the Western Territories was a guest. Bishop Joseph Talbot came from Indianapolis, Indiana, on a circuit tour of his jurisdiction.

At a breakfast for visitors Laura served "beefsteak, beat-biscuits, corn bread, hominy, toast, cold light bread and coffee with rich cream." Beat-biscuits, similar to ship's biscuit, were a Southern recipe reflecting her mother's Kentucky heritage. During preparation the baker beats the dough with a mallet.

Another dish Laura enjoyed preparing was Sally Lunn, a muffinlike coffee cake. From her kitchen, she turned out cakes, ginger snaps and apple fritters. She made Indian pudding, a dessert containing fresh or dried apples or other fruit, cornmeal and molasses.

BEFORE MOVING TO AURORA in 1862, Laura and Ramon Sanchez, left, posed for a San Francisco photographer wth Laura's sister Nannie, and father, Alexander P. Crittenden.

After one long day together, outdoors, Laura and Ramon had a late dinner, consisting of rice, beefsteak, lettuce, some leftover pudding, and coffee with soda crackers.

Through most of the year fruits

and vegetables were scarce in Aurora. Hens' eggs were expensive, when available. More common were gulls eggs from Mono Lake. Hunters brought in fat sage hens in summer. Fishermen provided fine trout from Walker River and its tributaries. In midsummer Laura said "splendid rich milk" was plentiful and inexpensive.

Because there was no sewing machine in the Sanchez home, Laura did all her sewing by hand. She darned socks and repaired dresses in the evening by the light of a kerosene lamp. After sewing curtains for the bedroom, she had enough red material left to make a cover for her dressing table.

She had to pay $4 a dozen for washing of skirts and dresses, $3 a dozen for all other large pieces, and 75 cents a dozen for handkerchiefs and napkins. It took several tries for Laura to find a satisfactory washerwoman for the weekly laundering.

During the winter food and all kinds of goods became scarce in the remote mountain town. Sometimes even ink to write letters was hard to come by. The arrival of the first pack train of the year, usually in late April, was a welcome event.

At the end of January 1865, the people of Aurora endured several days of snow, cold temperatures and high winds. Nearly a foot of snow fell. When the sun finally returned, many couples went sleigh-riding. Mr. and Mrs. Sanchez rented a sleigh and joined the fun. The jingling of the bells helped to cheer everyone's spirits after the spell of bad weather. When Ramon tried to make a tight turn he tipped over the sleigh. They landed in a heap, with Laura on top of Ramon, all mixed up with blankets and cushions. The horses stopped, and no harm was done.

Laura had a favorite green muslin dress that she often donned after completing her morning household work. She would pin up the dress and tie on a full apron to cook dinner. In the hot, dry, dusty weather of August she took off her underskirts – and promptly became chilled when the sun went down and the temperatures dipped close to freezing.

Eventually she found a girl, Lucinda, to help with household work. Laura insisted the girl attend school during the day. Lucinda's chores were to black the stove, wash up the kitchen floor and the back and front porches and keep the paint clean, each task to be done three times a week. She swept and dusted the master bedroom, parlor, hall, stairs and her own bedroom each day. Laura didn't trust Lucinda with the dishes or in her kitchen. They never became friends in the way Laura had felt close to the family maid, Mary, in San Francisco.

The first year, Laura and Ramon remained in Aurora until fall. They returned to San Francisco in time for the wedding of Laura's sister, Nannie, to Sidney VanWyck. Laura waited out the Sierra winter in warmer San Francisco. Ramon returned to Aurora in December. Laura joined him in June. That fall they moved to a new two-story brick house, where they remained through the next two winters.

THE SANCHEZ HOME, sketched from photos and other information.

The newly-wed Mr. and Mrs. VanWyck also came to Aurora, remaining about a year before moving to Virginia City. It was a pleasure to Laura to have her sister nearby.

The absence of an Episcopal minister in Aurora disappointed Laura. She liked the Rev. Mr. Yager of the Baptist Church personally, but felt his preaching was lacking in quality. Though they never had children of their own, Mr. and Mrs. Sanchez began holding Trinity Episcopal congregation's Sunday School in their home. Later they had about 50 children enrolled. Classes were moved to the Baptist Church building where four other teachers aided them.

The thriving town of Aurora was nestled at the confluence of two streams. Surrounded by three hills, there were no long views of the landscape. However, from the 9,300 foot summit of nearby Mt. Brawley, Laura reported, "you can see the surrounding country for miles and miles, and have a full view of Mono Lake." Ramon had often heard about the grandeur of the mountain scenery from that vantage point. One Saturday afternoon at the end of July they rented horses and made the ascent. Although both enjoyed riding, it was too costly to do often. Wildflowers were blooming in abundance on the mountaintop. They gathered a bouquet. At home, she put the flowers in a bowl, then put the bowl in a soup dish. When she set this on a small table, the flowers added a corner of color.

The couple often sat together on the porch in early summer evenings. Laura found the abundance of flying bugs to be a great annoyance during August and September.

Life in Aurora most days was very quiet for a woman at home alone. Laura kept busy in the house to avoid feeling lonely. Her husband's partner and his wife, Dr. and Mrs. J. L. Howard, lived across town. Though Laura enjoyed Mrs. Howard's company, they did not become close friends. The distance and the dusty walk involved kept them from meeting often. Laura was not part of the Ladies Sewing Circle or other ladies' community groups in Aurora. Because she sympathized with the Southern cause during those Civil War years, as her family and her husband did, she was at odds with many Aurorans.

Laura's brother-in-law, Sidney VanWyck, had a metal assaying business in town. Her younger brother, Howard, was also in Aurora. He sometimes dined at the Sanchez house, or at the VanWyck's. Howard found boarding at Louise's French Restaurant offered too few good things to eat. It was also plagued by too many flies. He was bookkeeper for the Wide West Gold and Silver Mining Co., but at 18 his dream was to join the Confederate Army, as had two older brothers. He also pined for the single young ladies he remembered from San Francisco.

In 1863 Laura's father, Alexander P. Crittenden, a respected attorney and former California legislator, came to visit his three children living in Aurora. The Real del Monte Mine hired him to defend it in the lawsuit initiated by the Pond Mining Company. Laura and Ramon's cozy brick home became the gathering place for the Crittenden kin when they were in Aurora.

The mine litigation took A. P. Crittenden to Carson City for a few months, then he opened a law office in Virginia City.

When spring came to Aurora in 1865, the boom was over. Many people who had gone elsewhere to winter failed to return. Others moved away. The banking business became very slow. Ramon was hired to be the Bodie representative of the New York-based Empire Gold and Silver Mining and Milling Company. He spent much of the spring there, supervising construction of a new mill. In the fall they moved to Virginia City, where Ramon Sanchez joined Sidney VanWyck in the assay business.

Laura Sanchez often wrote to her mother Clara, who remained in San Francisco. Writing letters to her mother and sister helped make up for her lack of close friends in town. A collection of many of her letters, along with other Crittenden family letters, is among the holdings at the William Clements Library at the University of Michigan. These letters provided the information presented here. It is used by permission.

Bibliographic Notes

One of the most revealing books on the history of both Aurora and Bodie is Roger D. McGrath's *Gunfighters Highwaymen and Vigilantes,* published by the University of California Press in 1984. McGrath focuses on the violent sides of both towns, and of the region in general. His bibliography is an excellent source list for both Aurora and Bodie.

J. Ross Browne provides a glimpse of the town's life in *A Trip to Bodie Bluff and the Dead Sea of the West,* first published in 1865, and since then in various reprints.

Information and list of residents and advertisements appear in J. Wells Kelly's *First Directory of the Nevada Territory.* A resident of Aurora, Colonel Samuel Youngs, kept a journal which was reprinted by the Nevada Historical Society in 1959. Youngs also provided information to Myron Angel for his *Thompson & West's History of Nevada 1881,* and to Kelley for his second directory. Youngs was correspondent for the Sacramento *Daily Union* for many years, and the articles he wrote from the town appear in that paper's columns during the 1860s and 1870s.

Another temporary resident, Samuel Clemens, included a view of daily life in Aurora in the classic volume *Roughing It,* written under that great name "Mark Twain." Many versions are available, most notably that of the University of California Press. The available letters from Clemens in Aurora are reprinted in an annotated volume of his *Letters,* also from the University of California Press.

A few editions of Aurora newspapers from the 1860s are available on microfilm at the Nevada State Library. The newspapers were the *Aurora Daily Times, Esmeralda Daily Union,* and *Esmeralda Star.* Over the years, Aurora was home at one time or another to six different newspapers.

As indicated, the Laura Sanchez letters are part of the larger Crittenden correspondence held by the William Clements Library, University of Michigan. The information here is used by permission of the Library. Recipes for Boston Brown Bread, beat, or beaten, biscuits and other breads mentioned in the text may be found in *Joy of Cooking,* by Irma S. Rombauer.

BOOKS ABOUT AURORA AND THE CALIFORNIA-NEVADA BORDER COUNTRY

NEVADA GHOST TOWNS & MINING CAMPS, by Stanley W. Paher. Large 8-1/2 x 11 format, 500 pages, 710 illus., maps, index. About 668 ghost towns are described with travel directions. It contains more pictures and describes more localities than any other Nevada book. Every page brings new information and unpublished photos of the towns, the mines, the people, and early Nevada life.

NEVADA GHOST TOWNS & MINING CAMPS ILLUSTRATED ATLAS, VOL. I – Northern Nevada: Reno - Austin - Ely, and points north. **VOL. II** – Southern Nevada, Death Valley - Mojave Desert. Each 104 pages, 7 x 10. Combined edition, 208 pages. Ghost towns and placer gold mining sites are located on 56 new maps. Also located are caves, gem sites, hot springs, old mines, state parks, recreation sites, 4x4 roads, trails.

BODIE...BOOM TOWN. GOLD TOWN! THE LAST OF CALIFORNIA'S OLD-TIME MINING CAMPS, by Douglas McDonald. 48 pages, illus., 7 x 10. Though Bodie was discovered in 1859, the height of the boom occurred in 1880, yet the mines were still active until 1920. Illustrations show the mines and miners, street scenes, buildings, the mill, bullion, and the crowds which made up Bodie.

BODIE BONANZA, by Warren Loose. 246 pages, illus. A Bodie native chronicles the social picture of the camp's heyday (1878-1880), lacing the text with news stories of fortunes, failures, rowdiness, business, "red lights," and entertainments. A closing chapter surveys later happenings at what is now Bodie State Park.

COMSTOCK MINING & MINERS, by Eliot Lord. 478 pages, illus., maps. This narrative history of the Comstock Lode traces the birth of the silver mining industry in turbulent Virginia City with much on day-to-day life, mining and milling techniques, and Comstock personalities. A landmark Nevada book.

NEVADA LOST MINES AND BURIED TREASURES, by Douglas McDonald. 128 pages, 6 x 9, illus. Legends of lost mines in Nevada date from thetime when westbound emigrants discovered silver in the desolate Black Rock Desert. The author recounts 74 stories and includes tales of buried coins, bullion bars, stolen bank money, etc. Maps show general treasure localities.

NEVADA TOWNS AND TALES, S. W. Paher, ed. 2 vols., 224 pages ea., 8-1/2 x 11. Chapters focus on economic, social, and geographic factors, state emblems, politics, mining, ghost towns, prospecting, legends, early day women, ranching, industries, transportation, etc. Indexed. Vol. 1, North; Vol. 2, South.

MINING DISTRICTS AND MINERAL RESOURCES OF NEVADA, by Francis C. Lincoln. 295 pages, maps, index. This compilation describes 307 districts,with historical summaries and bibliographies keyed to dozens of mining publications and journal articles through 1923. Mineral locations are also noted by types.

MINING CAMP DAYS, by Emil W. Billeb. 229 pages, illus. Provides insights into Nevada and eastern California mining camps after 1905. Dozens of unpublished photographs were taken by this observer-participant, augmenting a lively text.

JULIA BULETTE AND THE RED LIGHT LADIES OF NEVADA, by Douglas McDonald. 32 pages, illus., map. Here is the story of Virginia City's famed prostitute, who was murdered in 1867. An overview of Nevada prostitution occupies the last part of the book, augmented by interesting photographs.

THE BIG BONANZA, by Dan DeQuille (William Wright). 488 pages, illus., Indexed. Subtitled "An authentic account of the discovery, history, and working of the Comstock Lode," this book covers every phase of the epic rise of Virginia City, especially the special technology required to work the deep silver mines.

DEATH VALLEY GHOST TOWNS, VOL. I, AND VOL. II, by S. W. Paher. 32 pages ea., 9 x 12, map, 50 illus. Death Valley is known for its colorful eras of borax mining, as well as gold and silver rushes also. Includes Calico, Rhyolite, Greenwater, Panamint City—about 35 mining camps in all.

For further information, or to request a free catalog, write or call:

Nevada Publications

Box 15444 • Las Vegas, Nevada 89114 • (702) 747-0800